Bram Stoker

BRAM STOKER

THE MAN WHO WROTE *DRACULA*

STEVEN OTFINOSKI

FRANKLIN WATTS
A Division of Scholastic Inc.
New York Toronto London Auckland Sydney
Mexico City New Delhi Hong Kong
Danbury, Connecticut

Photographs © 2005: Art Resource, NY: 45 (Erich Lessing), 17 (Scala); Aurora/Voelkel/laif: 98; Bram Stoker Collection, Shakespeare Centre Library, Stratford-upon-Avon: 70; Bridgeman Art Library International Ltd., London/New York: 63 (Pierre Falke/Bibliotheque Nationale, Paris, France/Archives Charmet), 40 (John Atkinson Grimshaw/Christopher Wood Gallery, London, UK), 55 (Istvan Kolonics/Private Collection/Archives Charmet); Corbis Images: 24, 38, 51, 57, 71, 76, 80, 84 left, 89, 95 (Bettmann), 97 (Ed Bock), 74 (E. O. Hoppé), cover, 92 (Hulton-Deutsch Collection), 47 (Jose Fuste Raga), 21, 22 (Sean Sexton Collection), back cover ghost (Grant Smith), 93 (Underwood & Underwood), 66 (Florence Vandamm/Condé Nast Archive); Everett Collection: 91, 94; Getty Images: 27, 78 (Herbert Barraud/Hulton Archive), 52 (Alexander Bassano/Time Life Pictures), 83 (Blank Archives/Hulton Archive), 84 right (Fotos International/Hulton Archve), 8, 14, 34, 49, 60, 65, 86 (Hulton Archive), 100 (John Kobal Foundation/Hulton Archive), 2 (Time Life Pictures); Kobal Collection/Picture Desk/Universal: 88; Library of Congress: 64; Mary Evans Picture Library: 68 (Tony Grubhofer), 11, 73; North Wind Picture Archives: 13, 36; Peter Arnold Inc./Hans Madej/Bilderberg: 42; Reprinted with permission from Bram Stoker: A Biography of the Author of Dracula by Barbara Belford, Knopf, 1996: 6 left, 6 right, 10, 30; The Art Archive/Picture Desk/Matthew Brady/National Archives, Washington, D.C.: 19; The Image Works/Topham: 96.

Library of Congress Cataloging-in-Publication Data

Otfinoski, Steven.

  Bram Stoker : the man who wrote Dracula / by Steven Otfinoski.

    p. cm. — (Great life stories)

  Includes bibliographical references and index.

  ISBN 0-531-16750-X

  1. Stoker, Bram, 1847–1912—Juvenile literature. 2. Novelists, English—19th century—Biography—Juvenile literature. 3. Theatrical managers—Great Britain—Biography—Juvenile literature. 4. Dracula, Count (Fictitious character)—Juvenile literature. I. Title. II. Series.

  PR6037.T617Z815 2005

  823'.8—dc22   2005000374

CONTENTS

Abraham (later Bram) Stoker was the third child born to Abraham Stoker (left) and his wife, Charlotte (right).

ONE

A Sickly Childhood

Clontarf, Ireland, is a tiny village along the wild Irish coast, just 3 miles (4.8 kilometers) north of Dublin. Small in size, Clontarf is rich in history and legend, and a dark history it is. For centuries, it was a hideout for smugglers, cutthroats, and murderers. Behind these real villains there lurked supernatural ones as well. These included ghosts, demons, and those wailing Irish spirits known as banshees.

On November 8, 1847, a third son was born in Clontarf to Abraham Stoker, a civil servant, and his wife, Charlotte. They named him Abraham, after his father, a name he later shortened to Bram.

A DISTINGUISHED FAMILY

The Stokers were middle-class, Anglo-Irish Protestants. Abraham's ancestors had come to Ireland from England in the seventeenth century. The island nation had been under English control since 1541, and many Englishmen went to Ireland to acquire land and make their fortune. Many of the Stokers became doctors and medical researchers. Young Abraham's uncle William was a doctor, and three of his brothers would become doctors. His mother's family, the Thornleys, were less distinguished but more colorful. They were tradespeople and soldiers. In 1798, a group of Irish patriots, known as the Society of United Irishmen, started a rebellion

In the 1840s, when Abraham Stoker met Charlotte Thornley, Dublin was a bustling but very poor city. Above, Trinity College is located at the end of College Street.

against the English. Among the rebels was Abraham's maternal great-granduncle. When the rebellion failed, he was hanged by the English.

Abraham Stoker worked from the age of sixteen in the Chief Secretary's Office in Dublin Castle. Despite its name, Dublin Castle was actually a group of buildings dating back to 1224 that had served over the centuries as a fort, a prison, and a courthouse. Abraham was a confirmed bachelor of forty-five when he met the vivacious twenty-five-year-old Charlotte Thornley on a vacation in 1844. They married and eventually had seven children.

DUBLIN

Dublin, the capital of the Republic of Ireland, is a city rich in history, much of it violent. Invading Vikings from Denmark established a settlement there in the 800s. It was seized by the English in 1170. Two years later Henry II of England named Dublin the seat of English government in Ireland, which the English then controlled. There were bloody uprisings from the 1200s through the 1800s, but the Irish received some independence in 1921 after an agreement with the English. The country did not fully break away from England until 1949.

During Bram Stoker's lifetime, Dublin was a city in decay. It was riddled with some of the worst slums in Europe. Despite economic woes, its spirit was strong. It was the birthplace and home to a number of famous Irish-Anglo writers. Among them were satirist Jonathan Swift, playwrights Oscar Wilde and George Bernard Shaw, and novelist Sheridan Le Fanu. Le Fanu was the author of the popular vampire tale *Carmilla,* which surely influenced the work of Bram Stoker.

Bram Stoker had his first photograph taken when he was seven.

AN UNKNOWN ILLNESS

Young Abraham Stoker was a sickly child. The specific ailment he suffered from was never revealed in his personal writings. His illness kept him virtually bedridden for the first seven or eight years of his life. He once claimed he could not stand upright without the help of others until he was seven.

The young invalid spent his days lying in bed, reading storybooks, and staring out his bedroom window at the often-stormy waters of Dublin Bay. The self-educated Charlotte taught Abraham and his sister Matilda and brother Thornley at home. She planted a love of learning in each of them. In the evenings, Charlotte Stoker would sit by Abraham's bedside and tell him Irish legends and myths that she had grown up hearing. She thrilled the small boy with frightening tales of fairies who drank the blood of children and of the banshee, a demon whose terrible wail signaled a coming death.

Some of these tales of terror were distressingly real. Charlotte Stoker told her spellbound son how as a girl she had survived the terrible cholera epidemic of 1832 that killed thousands. During the first two years of Bram's life, Ireland was struck with a famine that took as many as 1 million lives. The Stokers moved away from disease-ridden Dublin during the famine to breathe the healthier air of Clontarf. The elder Stoker's secure position in the government assured that they would not starve as many poor farming families did.

Yet for the family's sickly son, death remained a constant threat. "When the nursery bell rang at night," Stoker wrote years later, "my mother would run to the room expecting to find me dying."

The Stoker's fled famine-ridden Dublin to live in the seacoast town of Clontarf.

THE GREAT POTATO FAMINE

The Irish Potato Famine of 1845 to 1850 was one of the worst natural disasters in world history. The majority of Irish people at the time were poor farmers who relied on their potato crop as a staple food. When a disease ruined the crop, hundreds of thousands died from slow starvation. Those who ate the rotten crop got sick, and many of them died as well. As many as 2 million Irish people fled the country and emigrated to the United States and other countries, where they hoped to start new and better lives. From 1845 to 1851, the nation's population decreased from 8 million to 5 million people.

The potato famine changed Ireland in at least two important ways. Irish nationalism blossomed as many people blamed the English, who controlled the land and responded slowly to the crisis. Pressure from the Irish forced the English to pass new laws to protect the rights of Irish tenants living on property owned by English landowners. Also, agricultural production shifted from a reliance on one crop, potatoes, to a variety of crops to prevent another such catastrophe.

The dreadful misery of those dark years are summed up in this stanza from a poem, "The Song of the Famine," published in the *Dublin University Magazine* in July 1847:

Death! death! death!
In land and alley and street,
Each hand is skinny that holds the bier [a platform for carrying a coffin],
And totters each bearer's feet;
The livid faces mock their woe.
And the eyes refuse a tear,
For Famine's gnawing at every heart,
And tramples on love and fear!

A MIRACULOUS RECOVERY

Young Abraham Stoker, however, didn't die. "This early weakness passed away," he later wrote, "and I grew into a strong boy and in time enlarged to the biggest member of my family." Much to everyone's surprise, Stoker became a vigorous and athletic youth. At age twelve, he entered the Reverend William Woods's preparatory school in Dublin's Rutland Square. There he took classical subjects such as Latin that would prepare him for college. He also distinguished himself in the sport of endurance walking. When he graduated four years later, Stoker was a tall, hand-some, red-haired lad brimming with energy and confidence.

Despite this, he would never forget his early years as a bedridden invalid, with death hovering over him. Nor would he forget the tales of horror that his mother had told him. They would haunt his imagination for the rest of his life.

Bram Stoker's writing was influenced by his mother's stories of blood-drinking fairies and banshees (such as the one at the right) as well as his childhood brush with death.

At Trinity College, Bram Stoker excelled in sports, but not in academics.

Gollege and a Gareer

In 1863, Stoker entered Trinity College, also known as the University of Dublin, one of Ireland's most prestigious universities. If Stoker grew at prep school, he positively blossomed at Trinity. He quickly became one of the college's outstanding athletes, excelling at rugby, rowing, weight lifting, and long-distance walking. He would be a daily walker all his life. In 1867, he was named University Athlete, a title that went to the best all-around sportsman on campus. That same year he won awards in the 5- and 7-mile (8- and 11-km) walk, and weight lifting.

A PASSION FOR POETRY AND DEBATING

His success on the playing field brought the once withdrawn youth out of his shell. "My big body and athletic prowess gave me a certain position in which I had to overcome my natural shyness," he later wrote.

Stoker was invited to join the Philosophical Society and the Historical Society, the two most distinguished student organizations at Trinity. The Philosophical Society encouraged its members to read aloud papers on various academic subjects and issues of the day. The Historical Society was a debating group. Through these organizations, Stoker became a skillful debater and an effective public speaker. He would eventually become president of the Philosophical Society.

TRINITY COLLEGE

The oldest and most prestigious institute of higher learning in Ireland, Trinity College was founded in 1592 under a charter granted by Queen Elizabeth I of England. During Stoker's days there, Trinity experienced some of its greatest growth. The college was attended exclusively by Protestant males. Catholics were not allowed to attend for another decade, and women were not admitted until 1904. Today, students from seventy countries attend the college, studying in one of six major areas. Two of the most prominent features of the college are the Oscar Wilde Centre for Irish Writing and the Samuel Beckett Centre and Theatre named for two Irish-born playwrights.

Although he received honors in mathematics, his best subject, Stoker was not a top student. He never received a scholarship to Trinity, as two of his brothers had. He was more interested in after-hours gab sessions with his fellow students at the local pub than in classroom discussion. He loved to while the night away, drinking and discussing contemporary issues and the theater, which he attended frequently with his father. He also had a passion for poetry. His favorite poets were the great early nineteenth-century English Romantics—John Keats, Percy Bysshe Shelley, and Lord George Gordon Byron. He was attracted to their celebration of the individual and their love of nature.

The poet Percy Bysshe Shelley is known as one of England's great poets. In 1816, he married Mary Wollstonecraft, who later wrote *Frankenstein*.

A CIVIL SERVANT

In 1865, Stoker's father, having attained the position of first-class clerk, retired from the civil service after nearly half a century. It was his desire that his son Abraham follow him in the civil service just as he had followed his own father's career. Stoker took a leave of absence from Trinity and worked as a clerk at Dublin Castle for a year. He then returned to college and graduated from Trinity in 1871 with a science degree. Despite his desire for a more exciting profession, Stoker dutifully accepted his father's wishes and entered the civil service as a full-time clerk.

The work was steady and the income sufficient, but Stoker longed for the glamour of the theater. His favorite actor was a rising star of the British theater, Henry Irving, who brought a new realism and excitement to the stage. For a time, Stoker worked as an actor, playing minor roles in comedies and farces, mostly in productions of the Trinity College Dramatic Society. He also stayed active in the Philosophical Society, regularly speaking on various topics, such as poetry, William Shakespeare, and women's rights.

A DRAMA CRITIC

Stoker soon felt his gift was more with the written word than with the spoken word. He was disappointed that the city's leading newspaper, the *Dublin Evening Mail,* did not regularly review the productions starring Henry Irving that he so enjoyed. In November 1871, he decided to do something about it. He applied to the *Evening Mail* for the position of theater critic. He got the job, but it was hardly a prestigious position. Stoker received no salary and was not even given credit for his writing, but the young reviewer didn't care. It was enough for him to be writing about the theater and seeing his words in print. With his university degree, Stoker was the most educated theater critic in Dublin. He was probably the only reviewer in Ireland who actually read each play before seeing it. His insightful reviews, especially of Henry Irving's work, were well received by the public.

Stoker had another hero besides Irving. While at Trinity he read a British edition of the American poet Walt Whitman's book of poems *Leaves of Grass.* Whitman was a bold new voice in contemporary poetry. He wrote most of his poems in unmetered, free verse that didn't rhyme and celebrated his independent spirit and that of the democratic United States. In February 1872, Stoker wrote a long, admiring letter to Whitman that revealed as much about himself as it did his love of Whitman's poetry.

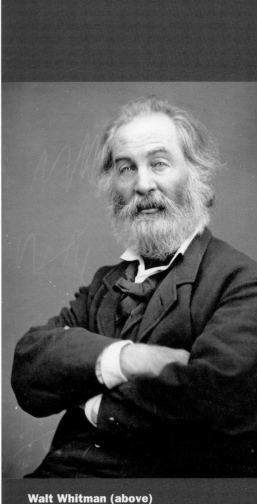

Walt Whitman (above) was photographed by the famous Civil War photographer Matthew Brady. Whitman was deeply influenced by his own war experiences tending wounded soldiers in Washington, D.C.

"I am ugly but strong and determined and have a large bump over my eyebrows," he wrote. "I have a heavy jaw and a big mouth and thick—sensitive nostrils—a snub nose and straight hair. . . . I am equal in temper and cool in disposition and have a large amount of self control and am naturally secretive to the world." Although he did not have the courage to send this first letter to Whitman, he did write and mail another one. Soon the young Irish civil servant and the middle-aged American poet struck up a long correspondence that ended with Whitman's death years later.

WALT WHITMAN

Today, Walt Whitman is considered a great American poet. When he first tried to publish his book *Leaves of Grass,* however, no publisher thought it worthy of print. Whitman grew up in Brooklyn, New York, and worked as a printer and journalist before turning to poetry. Along the way he pursued other jobs. He worked for a time as a carpenter, teacher, and editor of the newspaper the *Brooklyn Eagle.*

After many rejections of his poetry collection, Whitman finally published *Leaves of Grass* at his own expense in 1855. Most U.S. critics called the book vulgar and immoral. The poet received his first recognition in Great Britain, where writers such as the young Abraham Stoker praised his groundbreaking work. Whitman continued to revise and enlarge *Leaves of Grass* until shortly before his death, in 1892. His bold poems that sang of U.S. democracy and the importance of the self continue to inspire readers today.

That same year, 1872, Stoker's parents and sisters left Ireland for France and Switzerland, where they could live more cheaply on father Abraham's modest pension. They moved frequently from place to place. Back home in Ireland, Stoker enjoyed his freedom from parental restraints and turned his thoughts toward a full-time career as a writer.

Dublin was a large city by the 1870s. Its population rose during the potato famine, when many of the starving fled to the city.

Stoker wrote his first book, a handbook for clerks, while working at Dublin Castle (above).

THREE

UNDER HENRY IRVING'S SPELL

By 1873, Stoker's life could not have been busier. His days were spent clerking at Dublin Castle. His nights were spent regularly attending the theater and writing reviews. In whatever spare time he had, Stoker worked on a master's degree in mathematics at Trinity, which took him three years to complete. He also found time to begin writing stories for pleasure and a little extra income. He had sold his first story, "The Crystal Cup," a fantasy, to *London Society* magazine the previous year.

IN DUBLIN'S SOCIAL WHIRL

Although Abraham Stoker Sr. loved the theater as much as his son did, he had a low opinion of actors. This was common at the time. Actors were considered to be at the low end of the social scale. Abraham advised his son not to socialize with them, but Stoker disregarded this advice. He thoroughly enjoyed visiting the cast backstage after a performance and attending opening-night parties.

Through his job as a theater critic and his connections at Trinity, he became a regular at the Saturday night parties of one of Dublin's most eccentric and colorful couples—Sir William and Lady Jane Wilde. Stoker had gone to Trinity with the Wildes's son, Willie, and was also acquainted with their younger, highly gifted son Oscar. Sir William was a

Oscar Wilde is well-known for his witticisms. When asked to revise one of his plays, he said, "Who am I to tamper with a masterpiece?"

respected eye surgeon and author, but it was his wife who was the star of their parties. Lady Wilde dressed in outlandish clothes that made her look more like a gypsy queen than a lady aristocrat. She held court at her parties with a steady stream of witty and provocative pronouncements. It was a gift her son Oscar would inherit.

OSCAR WILDE

Seven years Bram Stoker's junior, Oscar Wilde soon proved that he could write as wittily as he spoke. Like Stoker's, his first published work was a collection of fairy tales, *The Happy Prince and Other Tales* (1888). Wilde's only novel, *The Picture of Dorian Gray* (1891), like Stoker's *Dracula,* is a classic of horror literature. It is the tale of a young man whose portrait slowly deteriorates, reflecting his moral corruption, while he himself remains young. In the end, Dorian Gray dies, and the picture returns to his youthful image while the real Dorian turns into the ugly monster he had become.

Wilde was also a playwright. His sparkling comedies of the 1890s remain stage classics today, especially *The Importance of Being Earnest* (1895), a brilliant mixture of intricate verbal comedy and physical farce.

That same year, at the peak of his career, a sex scandal erupted that ruined Wilde. He was arrested and endured a highly publicized trial. He was convicted and sentenced to two years in prison performing hard labor. A broken man in body and spirit, upon his release Wilde moved to France. There he spent his last years in self-imposed exile.

A DEATH AND A REBIRTH

The vibrant nightlife that Stoker enjoyed was in sharp contrast to his plodding days as a clerk in Dublin Castle. He worked dutifully, but felt little kinship with the dull bureaucrats who surrounded him. Critical of the unimaginative and wasteful way the civil service was run, Stoker expressed his criticisms and detailed his experiences in a book. It was published in 1878 under the dry-as-dust title *The Duties of Clerks of Petty Sessions in Ireland*. In it, Stoker advocated a better filing system and other clerical reforms. It was his first full-length published work.

On October 12, 1876, Stoker's father died near Naples, Italy, where the family had been staying. Stoker traveled to Italy to attend the funeral. His mother and sisters enjoyed their independent and relatively inexpensive life and decided not to return to Ireland. Soon after, Stoker shortened his name from Abraham to Bram, signaling a new period in his life.

A FATEFUL NIGHT

Bram Stoker didn't want to spend his life chained to a clerk's desk in the musty halls of Dublin Castle like his father and grandfather had before him. He yearned to be a full-time writer like his hero Walt Whitman. He imagined himself writing plays for the London stage.

In December 1876, he received an invitation to dine with the other hero in his life. Henry Irving had read Stoker's glowing and insightful review of his performance as Hamlet, from Shakespeare's tragedy, at Dublin's Theatre Royal. Irving played the lead role of Hamlet, a Danish prince who seeks to avenge the murder of his father by his uncle, the new king of Denmark. "Irving is in face and form of a type of strongly expressed individuality. . . ." Stoker wrote. "Irving's physical appearance sets him at once above his fellows as no common man; but his physique is somewhat too weak for the heavy work which he has to go through."

Irving was impressed enough by Stoker's review to invite the drama critic to his suite at the Shelbourne Hotel. The twenty-nine-year-old theater critic eagerly accepted the invitation. Irving, thirty-eight, charmed and mesmerized his young admirer, and the two talked about the theater and other matters until dawn. To Stoker's surprise, Irving shared with him his dream of operating his own theater in London and mounting his productions there.

Stoker left the Shelbourne in the early morning with his head spinning. In the weeks and months ahead, he was invited several more times to Irving's suite for informal gatherings and play readings.

Stoker and Irving (above) began a lifelong partnership on that fateful night at the Shelbourne Hotel.

HENRY IRVING

Henry Irving was born with the untheatrical name John Henry Brodribb in 1838. He suffered from a childhood stammer that caused him to speak with breaks and pauses that he couldn't control. Irving overcame the disability and became an actor. At age eighteen, the year he made his theatrical debut, he changed his name to Irving, in honor of the American writer Washington Irving. He had the rare gift of being able to make his audiences totally identify with the role he was playing, especially villainous ones. His most famous role was as the miserly, vengeful Shylock in Shakespeare's *The Merchant of Venice*. Although his acting was extremely romantic and at times melodramatic, Irving also brought an innovative realism to the stage. He insisted on correct detail in every prop, costume, and set. In 1895, at the height of his career, he became the first British actor to be honored with knighthood, granted by Queen Victoria.

ROMANCE

Among the large group of actors, writers, and artists Stoker met through Irving and the Wildes was Florence Balcombe, an aspiring actress and daughter of a lieutenant colonel who had served in British India. Stoker called her an "exquisitely pretty girl . . . just seventeen with the most perfectly beautiful face I ever saw." He was not alone in his admiration of Florence Balcombe. One writer called her one of the three loveliest women in England. Among her other admirers was Oscar Wilde, who would soon become a prominent author. At that time Stoker, with a steady job and stable habits, seemed the better catch for Florence, and the couple became engaged.

Henry Irving returned to Dublin in late 1877 to perform a repertory season. He shared with Stoker his scheme to lease the Lyceum Theatre in London and become, as other famous actors had before him, an actor-manager. He invited Stoker to join him, offering him the position of acting manager of the theater. His salary would be 22 pounds ($110) a week.

Stoker didn't have to think twice before accepting the offer. Here was an opportunity to become a real part of the world of the theater and go to work for the greatest living actor on the English stage. It was the fulfillment of his dream of working in the theater full-time. Stoker abruptly quit his civil service job, happily forfeiting his pension rights. His late father would have been appalled.

At the same time that he was embarking on a new career, Stoker was also beginning a new phase in his personal life. On December 4, 1878, he and Florence Balcombe were married. He was thirty-one, and she was nineteen. They skipped their honeymoon so that Stoker would have time to prepare for his new job at the Lyceum. The newlyweds moved into an apartment in London not far from the theater that would become the center of Bram Stoker's life.

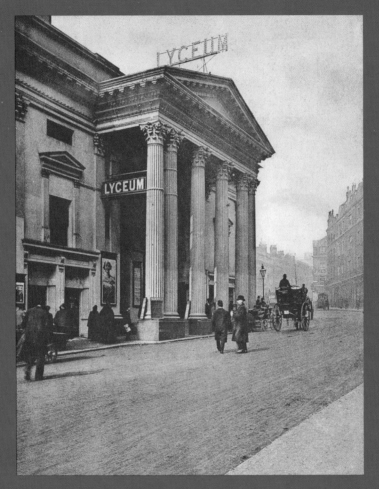

Under Irving and Stoker, the Lyceum Theatre rose to
national importance.

A Life in the Theater

London's Lyceum Theatre was one of the most popular playhouses in the city when Irving took it over. He quickly turned it into a sparkling showcase for his extraordinary talents as an actor and producer. Irving hired the beautiful actress Ellen Terry as his leading lady, along with a company of ninety actors and extras. Together Irving and Terry would become the leading couple of the British stage. Irving's productions of Shakespeare and contemporary plays were highlighted by sumptuous sets and dazzling costumes. No expense was spared to create a picture of realism. In his 1882 production of Shakespeare's *Romeo and Juliet,* Irving filled the stage with 135 extras and live peacocks in the

ELLEN TERRY

Ellen Terry was to the leading lady of the stage what Henry Irving was to the leading man. There was no one better. For nearly fifty years, Ellen Terry reigned as England's greatest actress.

She made her professional debut at age eight in Shakespeare's *Winter's Tale*. She played juvenile parts until her marriage at age sixteen to artist G. F. Watts, who was thirty years her senior. The marriage lasted only a year. Three years later she ran off with architect Edward Godwin and had two children. She left the stage for six years to care for them.

When she returned to the theater, Terry became famous for playing Shakespearean heroines. She brought intelligence and great beauty to the roles of Portia in *The Merchant of Venice* and Beatrice in *Much Ado About Nothing*. She was equally fine as the tragic figures of Desdemona in *Othello* and Lady Macbeth in *Macbeth*.

Terry and Henry Irving became the first couple of the London stage. She finally left his company after nearly twenty-five years and became manager of the Imperial Theatre where her son was set designer. She made her one appearance on film in 1917 in *Her Greatest Performance*. She gave her last regular stage performance in June 1919, playing Juliet's nurse in *Romeo and Juliet*. (In her younger days, she was a stunning Juliet.) In 1925, Terry was made a Dame of the British Empire, the female equivalent to receiving a knighthood. She died three years later.

"Ellen Terry is the most beautiful name in the world," wrote the Irish playwright George Bernard Shaw, whose plays she performed in. "It sings like a chime through the last quarter of the nineteenth century."

banquet scene. In his production of *Faust,* a play about a scholar who sells his soul to the devil, he filled the stage with 250 dancing demons and goblins and witches flying on broomsticks.

Irving did not work his theatrical magic alone. He was ably assisted by Stoker, his acting manager, and stage manager H. J. Loveday.

STOKER IN CHARGE

Stoker's official title of acting manager didn't begin to describe the many jobs he performed at the Lyceum. He supervised a house staff of forty-eight people, ran the box office, kept track of all expenses, and functioned as Irving's personal secretary. In this last capacity, he wrote all of Irving's off-stage speeches to various groups and organizations. He also wrote, by his own account, about half a million letters in Irving's name over twenty-seven years.

If Irving was an innovator in theatrical stagecraft, Stoker was no less an innovator in theatrical management. He was, according to Stoker biographer Barbara Belford, the first person in modern theater to promote upcoming productions with widespread advertising. He also pioneered giving patrons incentives to book shows in advance and numbering the theater's expensive seats. Each evening without fail Stoker, dressed smartly in a formal suit with a white tie and a jacket with long coattails, would greet the audience members as they entered the theater.

Stoker's devotion to Irving, whom he called "the Chief," was complete. He even convinced his brother George, a doctor, to move in with him and Florence and become the theater's consulting physician. When he and Florence had their first, and only child, on December 31, 1879,

Stoker named the boy Irving Noel Thornley Stoker. But his demanding job left him little time for his wife and son.

A typical day's work would begin in the late morning and run through the evening's performance. It continued after the show with a late supper shared with Irving and cast members, followed by talk that would often last until dawn. Irving so enjoyed his manager's company

This illustration depicts the interior of the Lyceum Theatre as it was in 1847.

that he insisted on having it until he was ready for sleep. Days would go by when Florence and son Irving would barely see Stoker. When Florence attended the theater, it was usually in the company of good friend and playwright-lyricist William S. Gilbert, half of the talented operetta team Gilbert and Sullivan. Years later, a resentful Irving Noel Stoker would drop the "Irving" from his name, unable to forget how the great actor "stole" his father from him in his childhood.

For all his dogged devotion, Irving often took Stoker for granted, as he did many of the people who worked so hard for him. Occasionally, Irving would publicly ridicule his manager in a way that deeply hurt the sensitive Stoker, yet he rarely complained.

The Lyceum Theatre

The theater that made Irving a world-famous actor was built in 1771 for exhibitions and concerts. It was first licensed as a theater in 1809 and was destroyed by fire in 1830. The new Lyceum that rose on the foundation was much grander, with a total of 1,500 seats.

It remained one of London's most popular theaters until 1939. Its last production was *Hamlet,* with the distinguished actor John Gielgud, Ellen Terry's great nephew, in the title role. The Lyceum became a dance hall after World War II, then underwent a major restoration. It reopened as a legitimate theater in 1996. Interestingly, one of the early plays staged at the Lyceum was *The Vampire,* based on one of the first vampire stories in English literature, written by John Polidori, a friend of Lord Byron, in 1819.

THE BUDDING AUTHOR

To supplement his income and perhaps provide him with an identity apart from Irving and the Lyceum, Stoker continued to write fiction. In 1882, he published *Under the Sunset,* a collection of eight fairy tales, which he dedicated to his son. These eerie stories of good against evil demonstrated Stoker's fascination with fantasy and horror. Among the best stories in the book is "The Invisible Giant," which describes a terrible plague not unlike the cholera epidemic his mother lived through as a child. The book received good reviews and was the start of a promising writing career for the thirty-five-year-old author.

Henry Irving and Ellen Terry played the leading roles in Tennyson's *The Cup,* produced at the Lyceum in 1881. The play ran for one hundred and thirty nights.

Bram Stoker, Hero

On September 14, 1882, Stoker was returning to the theater from his home in London's Chelsea section on a steamboat on the Thames River when he saw an elderly man jump off the ship. Without hesitation, he tore off his coat and dived into the churning waters. Stoker grasped the suicidal man and held his head above water until more help arrived on another boat. He then carried the unconscious man to his home, where his brother George, the physician, tried to revive him with mouth-to-mouth resuscitation. The unfortunate man, who was never identified, died. Stoker was awarded the Bronze Medal of the Royal Humane Society for his valiant efforts. Among those who praised Stoker's heroism was playwright Arthur Pinero. "How proud I am to count myself amongst those who have the privilege of your acquaintance," he wrote to Stoker in a letter.

Stoker was the mainstay of the Lyceum. Through his position he met and befriended many of England's leading celebrities, including artist James McNeill Whistler; author Sir Arthur Conan Doyle, creator of Sherlock Holmes; Prime Minister William Gladstone; and poet Alfred Lord Tennyson. Tennyson's play *The Cup* was produced at the Lyceum. Ellen Terry considered Stoker to be her rock in the difficult world of the theater. On occasion, when she felt some lines in a play they were staging weren't working, he would rewrite them for her. She affectionately called him her "nanny."

Like Walt Whitman, Mark Twain (above) had a powerful effect on American literature. He wrote the classics *Tom Sawyer* and *Huckleberry Finn*.

ON TOUR IN THE UNITED STATES

In late 1883, the entire Lyceum company made its first of six North American tours. With tons of sets and thousands of costumes to transport, the tour was an enormous undertaking and a daunting challenge to Stoker's exceptional organizational skills. Florence, who was becoming more and more estranged from her husband, remained at home with their son during the six-month tour.

Although he missed his family, Stoker enjoyed seeing the United States and its people, something he had dreamed about for years. In New York, he met and befriended Mark Twain, a writer who shared his interest in the strange and the occult. In Washington, D.C., he and other company members dined at the White House with President Chester Arthur. In March 1884, Stoker visited his hero, Walt Whitman, at his home in Camden, New Jersey. By then, Whitman was an old man with several ailments.

"His moustache is large and thick," Stoker later wrote of the old poet, "and fell over his mouth so as to mingle with the top of the mass of the bushy flowing beard." He would later use some of the same words to describe his most famous fictional creation, Count Dracula. Whitman took a great liking to Stoker, who he came to regard almost as a son. He did, however, take him to task for not keeping the strong, biblical name he was born with, Abraham.

A FIRST NOVEL

The company's first U.S. tour was so successful that they returned the following year. In what spare time he could find, Stoker continued to write. In 1890, he published his first novel, *The Snake's Pass,* a romantic adventure story set in Ireland. It revolved around the relationship between an English landlord and a Celtic peasant girl. It was the only one of his novels that Stoker set in his native country. *The Snake's Pass* was not as well-received as his earlier story collection. Like most of Stoker's subsequent novels, it was written quickly in the creative heat of the moment, with little refining or editing. These working habits gave much of Stoker's prose a sloppy, slapdash quality that earned him poor reviews from many book critics.

This was not the case with his next novel, which consumed nine years of his life and proved to be his one enduring masterpiece.

Whitby gained fame as a setting in *Dracula*. But the port is also known as the place where Captain James Cook's famous ships *Endeavor* and *Resolution* were built.

FIVE

The Genesis of Dracula

toker's idea of writing a novel about a vampire evolved slowly. According to his son, the thought may have begun with a dream he had after eating crab for supper. In the dream, he claimed he saw "a vampire king rising from the tomb to go about his ghastly business."

In 1890, Stoker spent three weeks on vacation with Florence and Noel in Whitby, a seaside resort and fishing village on the North Sea. There he began to make his first notes on the novel that would become *Dracula*. He would write much of the novel at Whitby and use the village as one of the book's key settings.

Stoker took his time with Dracula, thoroughly researching every aspect of the story and carefully and painstakingly structuring the plot. It is as if Stoker knew he had a great tale to tell and was prepared to handle it with the care and attention it demanded. *Dracula* is not only Stoker's best and most popular book, it is the only one still widely read today.

RESEARCHING VAMPIRES

Stoker did most of his research on *Dracula* at the British Museum Reading Room, where he pored over articles and books on the vampire lore of Eastern Europe. Vampires are undead creatures who rise at night from their graves to attack the living and drink their blood, thereby transforming their unfortunate victims into vampires as well.

Stoker was especially influenced by *The Land Beyond the Forest: Facts, Figures & Fancies from Transylvania,* a book written by historian and traveler Emily Gerard. A mountainous region that belonged to Hungary for a thousand years, Transylvania is now part of Romania. This remote area, "one of the wildest and least known parts of Europe," according to Stoker, was rich in superstitions, particularly those concerning vampires, which were terrifyingly real to the peasants who lived there.

Transylvania is known for its magnificent castles. Hunyadi Castle (left) was built in the fifteenth century.

Vampire Lore

"Vampires have appeared almost everywhere that men and women have bled," wrote *Dracula* scholar Leonard Wolf. Vampires are part of the folklore and superstitions of many nations and cultures, but they are particularly rich in Eastern Europe and Transylvania. Here are some of the folk beliefs concerning vampires that Stoker incorporated into Dracula.

- Vampires can only roam the earth at night. During the day they sleep in their coffins, which are filled with the earth they were originally buried in.

- Vampires can be warded off with a crucifix, the Christian Bible, holy water, and garlic.

- Vampires cast no image in a mirror.

- Vampires are able to transform themselves into bats, wolves, dogs, and other creatures at will.

- People who commit suicide or are condemned by a church are particularly prone to becoming vampires.

- A vampire can only be destroyed by having a wooden stake driven through its heart and then having its head cut off.

It is interesting to note that Stoker changed the "rules" of vampire lore when it suited his purpose. For instance, several times in his novel Count Dracula is seen walking about in daylight, and he is finally killed not with a wooden stake but with two sharp knives.

Another possible source of vampire lore for Stoker was Arminius Vambery, a visiting professor from the University of Budapest, Hungary, who may have told him about a historical figure from the Transylvania region who gave the writer both a name and personality for his antihero. An antihero is a central character in a work of fiction who is not a conventional hero, a definition that the evil Count Dracula certainly fills.

VLAD THE IMPALER

Vlad Tepes was a fifteenth-century prince of Wallachia, a region south of Transylvania, and a member of a dynasty that ruled the region for nearly four centuries. His father was Vlad Dracul, meaning "Vlad the Dragon or Devil." The son called himself "Dracula," meaning "Son of the Dragon."

Vlad was a cruel and violent man, even for the violent times he lived in. Wallachia and much of Eastern Europe in his day was being invaded by the Ottoman Turks, nomadic tribes that migrated to the Middle East and then Eastern Europe from Central Asia. As a teenager Vlad and his younger brother were held hostage by the Turks. When his father entered into an alliance with the Turks, he was murdered by former allies, along with Vlad's older brother. After being released by the Turks, Vlad came to power in Wallachia in 1448.

There is no historical evidence whatsoever linking Vlad to vampirism. He was not a supernatural being and never drank human blood, although he certainly enjoyed watching it be spilt. Vlad's cruelty is legendary. "Tepes" in his native tongue means "impaler," and he lived up to that grim name. Impalement, the piercing of the body with a pointed stick or stake, was his favorite form of execution. He took sadistic pleasure in watching his victims, impaled on a stake planted in the earth, die slowly, their bodies writhing in pain. According to the historical record, Vlad would dine on the killing field, amid the twisting bodies, enjoying a meal as he watched the slow deaths of his victims.

If Vlad only tortured Turks, the enemies of Christian Europe, he would be considered a hero, but he also victimized neighboring

The cruelty of Vlad Tepes confirms that some horror stories come from history books.

Romanians, Germans, and Hungarians. No one, not even his own nobles, was safe from his sadistic behavior. During a dinner amid his impaled victims, one of his nobles complained about the terrible stench coming from the dying and the dead. Vlad immediately ordered the noble to be impaled on a stake higher than the others. "That way you won't be so bothered by the smell below you," he told the unfortunate noble.

In 1462, Vlad was taken prisoner by King Mathias of Hungary and spent the next twelve years in captivity. Always crafty, Vlad managed to woo and marry Mathias's sister and converted from Orthodox Christianity to Roman Catholicism. Mathias granted him his freedom in 1474, and he was returned to power in Wallachia two years later. His last reign was blessedly brief. In a battle against the Turks, Vlad was killed. Some histories claim he disguised himself as a Turk to escape capture and was mistakenly killed by his own soldiers.

VLAD AND THE SULTAN'S ENVOYS

There are many stories of Vlad the Impaler's cruelty and his twisted sense of humor. One of the most famous concerns a visit of the Turkish sultan's envoys, or ambassadors, to his court. As they approached Vlad, they refused to remove their turbans as a sign of respect. They explained that doing so was against the laws of their Muslim religion. Furious at this slight, Vlad replied, "I will hammer in your law." He then ordered his men to hammer small nails into each envoy's head, nailing down their turbans.

Fascinated by the bloody deeds of the historical Dracula, Stoker borrowed his name and some of his background for his central character. He also appropriated Vlad's castle, moving it from Wallachia to Transylvania along the fabled Borgo Pass, the opening setting of his novel.

Bran Castle is sometimes called Dracula's Castle, but the historical Dracula never resided here.

ANOTHER MODEL FOR DRACULA

Vlad and the vampires of Transylvania were two models for Dracula. A third model was much closer to home for Stoker. Many historians and critics have pointed to Henry Irving as the most important model for Dracula. Irving was famous for portraying villainous characters on the stage. He was the devilish Mephistopheles in *Faust,* and a guilt-ridden murderer in his stirring recitation of Thomas Hood's poem "The Dream of Eugene Aram." More importantly, Irving controlled Stoker's existence and kept him from having a normal family life. In a sense Irving sucked the life out of Stoker, just as Dracula sucked life-giving blood from his victims. While Stoker allowed himself to be used by Irving and rarely said an unkind word about him, he harbored deep resentments. The writing of Dracula may have been his ultimate revenge on the larger-than-life figure who so dominated his life.

THE SHORT STORY WRITER

Working on *Dracula* had a good effect on Stoker's other writing. During these years, he produced some of his best and most frightening short stories. "Burial of the Rats" (1891) is a first-person account of a young Englishman adrift in Paris whose fascination with the sordid part of the city almost gets him killed by a legion of derelict cutthroats. The story's eerie atmosphere is heightened by the rats that scuttle about everywhere he looks, devouring corpses and leaving only the bones behind.

In "The Judge's House," published the same year, a young man named Malcolmson moves into a house haunted by the spirit of its previous owner, a judge. The judge was infamous for sentencing to the gallows many of the criminals who came before him. The dead man's spirit takes the form of a huge rat that races up and down a bell rope, the same rope once used to hang the condemned. In the shuddering climax, the ghostly judge returns to life and takes vengeance on Malcolmson, who has invaded his home:

> He felt the Judge's icy fingers touch his throat as he adjusted the rope. The noose tightened—tightened. Then the Judge, taking the rigid form of the student in his arms, carried him over and placed him standing in the oak chair, and stepping up beside him, put his hand up and caught the end of the swaying rope of the alarm bell. As he raised his hand the rats fled squeaking, and disappeared through the hole in the ceiling. Taking the end of the noose which was round Malcolmson's neck he tied it to the hang-bell rope, and then descending pulled away the chair.

Henry Irving played Mephistopheles in his 1885 production of Goethe's *Faust.* Mephistopheles tempts the title character to sell his soul.

Bram Stoker's Scariest Story

"The Squaw," published in 1893, ranks as Stoker's most disturbing work of fiction. It begins as a newlywed English couple tour a medieval castle in Nürnberg, Germany, with their American friend, Elias Hutcheson. The American unintentionally kills a kitten below the castle wall with a rock in sight of its mother.

> The black cat cast a swift upward glance, and we saw her eyes like green fire fixed an instant on Elias P. Hutcheson; and then her attention was given to the kitten, which lay still with just a quiver of her tiny limbs, whilst a thin red stream trickled from a gaping wound. With a muffled cry, . . . she bent over the kitten, licking its wound and moaning. Suddenly she seemed to realise that it was dead, and again threw her eyes up at us. . . . Her green eyes blazed with lurid fire, and the white, sharp teeth seemed to almost shine through the blood which dabbled her mouth and whiskers.

The tension builds as the vengeful cat follows the three humans around the grounds. Later, inside the castle, Hutcheson steps inside a torture chamber (pictured far right). The cat leaps like a demon from hell onto the museum worker holding open the door. The worker releases the door, and it snaps shut on the helpless man inside.

The story's last lines are delivered by the Englishman:

> And sitting on the head of the poor American was the cat, purring loudly as she licked the blood which trickled through the gashed socket of his eyes.
>
> I think no one will call me cruel because I seized one of the old executioner's swords and shore her in two as she sat.

One of Stoker's most gruesome tales is also one of his funniest. He wrote "The Dualitists; or, The Death Doom of the Double Born," with tongue in cheek for the Christmas edition of *Theatre* magazine several years before he began writing Dracula. It is the grisly story of child twins captured and tormented by two irredeemable juvenile delinquents. In the story's climax, the desperate twins' father attempts to shoot the tormentors off a roof but misses and shoots off the heads of his own children instead. The bloody corpses fall on their parents, killing them as well. The two guilty parties get off scot-free while the mother and father are accused posthumously of both infanticide and suicide. In a reference to the vampire lore that Stoker would soon immerse himself in, they "had stakes driven through their middles to pin them down in their unhallowed graves till the Crack of Doom."

The iron maiden is widely known as a medieval torture device, but was probably not invented until after the Middle Ages.

Wilkie Collins was an English writer who is considered by many to be the father of the English detective story.

SIX

ENTER THE COUNT

Dracula's format is an intriguing one. The entire novel is told in letters, journal entries, newspaper articles, and other forms of written correspondence and communication. This epistolary form was not uncommon in English novels of the eighteenth century. In fact, *Pamela,* written in 1739 by Samuel Richardson, is in epistolary form and is considered the first modern English novel. The writer Wilkie Collins, credited along with Edgar Allan Poe with creating the detective story, used the form in his 1860 mystery novel *The Woman in White.* The form of this novel is believed to have influenced Stoker heavily.

A CLASSIC PLOT

Dracula opens with a solicitor's agent, Jonathan Harker, en route to the Transylvanian castle of Count Dracula, a nobleman who is looking to relocate to London, England. When Harker first meets him, Count Dracula physically bears little resemblance to most of the movie Draculas to come. He does bear a striking resemblance to Henry Irving and Stoker's other hero, Walt Whitman.

Here is how he is described by Harker in his journal:

> Within, stood a tall old man, clean shaven save for a long white moustache, and clad in black from head to foot, without a single speck of colour about him anywhere. . . . The old man motioned me in with his right hand with a courtly gesture, saying in excellent English, but with a strange intonation: —"Welcome to my house! Enter freely and of your own free will!"

This last line of dialogue has a sinister tone. Vampires, according to European lore, cannot lure a person into their lairs unless they enter of their own free will. Indeed, Harker soon realizes to his horror that he is not Dracula's guest but his prisoner. These first four chapters contain some of the most gripping writing in the novel, including an eerie scene in which Harker is about to be assaulted by three female vampires, Dracula's "brides," before Dracula arrives on the scene:

> Never did I imagine such wrath and fury, even to the demons of the pit. His eyes were positively blazing. The red light in them

was lurid, as if the flames of hell-fire blazed behind them. His face was deathly pale, and the lines of it were hard like drawn wires; the thick eyebrows that met over the nose now seemed like a heaving bar of white-hot metal. With a fierce sweep of his arm, he hurled the woman from him, and then motioned to the others, as though he was beating them back; it was the same imperious gesture that I had seen used to the wolves. In a voice which, though low and almost in a whisper seemed to cut through the air and then ring in the room he said: —

"How dare you touch him, any of you? How dare you cast eyes on him when I had forbidden it? Back, I tell you all! This man belongs to me!"

Dracula isn't always depicted as an old man with a white mustache, although Stoker wrote him that way.

In another unforgettable scene Harker watches in horror from a window as Dracula creeps down the wall of his castle like some loathsome lizard. The count eventually leaves for England on a ship to claim his new estate and begin looking for fresh victims in the crowded city of London. Harker later manages to escape from the castle.

The action switches to England and involves Harker's fiancée Mina Murray, and her childhood friend, Lucy Westenra, a blonde beauty who is modeled on Stoker's wife, Florence. Mina, a more serious-minded working girl, is probably modeled on Stoker's beloved mother, Charlotte. Harker, with his well-organized mind, is undoubtedly modeled on Stoker himself. One of Lucy's three suitors is Dr. John Seward, who operates a sanatorium. The other two suitors are Arthur Holmwood, heir of an aristocratic family, and Quincey P. Morris, Stoker's version of an American cowboy. Renfield, a madman who enjoys catching and eating flies and other small creatures, is one of Seward's patients. Renfield is perhaps the most intriguing character in *Dracula,* a tormented soul who has a strange bond with Dracula, whom he calls his "master."

DRACULA IN ENGLAND

Mina and Lucy go to Whitby, where Lucy becomes engaged to Holmwood. During their stay, the ship carrying Count Dracula and fifty coffins of Transylvanian earth, in which he must sleep each day, arrives in the harbor. The entire ship's crew is dead or missing, including the captain, whose lifeless body is tied to the wheel. Dracula's systematic murder of the crew is grimly related in the captain's log and is another horrific highlight of the novel.

The count has taken the shape of a dog to slip off the ship and is not seen again until quite late in the novel. His first victim on English soil is Lucy, whom he visits nightly to drink her blood. Alarmed at Lucy's condition, Seward sends for his old college professor Abraham Van Helsing. Van Helsing is a superman of science who Stoker may have based partly on his father. After studying the case and finding small puncture marks on Lucy's neck, Van Helsing realizes that Lucy is the victim of a vampire. Despite his brave efforts to save her, she eventually dies and turns into a vampire herself. She is seen in a city park preying on young children.

Van Helsing, with the help of Seward, Holmwood, Morris, and Harker, who has returned safely from Transylvania, tracks Lucy to her coffin. In perhaps the most disturbing scene of the novel, Van Helsing convinces Holmwood, her former fiancée, to finish off the vampire who possesses Lucy's body and restore her to eternal peace:

Arthur placed the point over the heart, and as I looked I could see its dint [dent] in the white flesh. Then he struck with all his might.

Traditionally, a vampire can only be killed with a stake through the heart, followed by beheading.

The Thing in the coffin writhed; and a hideous, blood-curdling screech came from the opened red lips. The body shook and quivered and twisted in wild contortions. The sharp white teeth champed together till the lips were cut, and the mouth was smeared with a crimson foam. But Arthur never faltered. . . .

And then the writhing and quivering of the body became less, and the teeth ceased to champ, and the face to quiver. Finally it lay still. The terrible task was over.

With Lucy gone, Dracula turns his bloodthirsty attention to Mina. Van Helsing uses information given to him by Harker to track down forty-nine of the fifty coffins. He "defiles" them by placing the Holy Eucharist, a small wafer of consecrated bread used in the Christian rite of Communion, inside each. Realizing his days are numbered if he remains in England, Dracula flees to Transylvania with his one remaining coffin. Van Helsing and his young assistants pursue him. En route to his castle, Count Dracula is finally destroyed in his coffin as daylight wanes, not with a wooden stake but with two large knives:

The sun was almost down on the mountaintops, and the shadows of the whole group fell long upon the snow. I saw the Count lying within the box upon the earth, some of which the rude falling from the cart had scattered over him. He was deathly pale, just like a waxen image, and the red eyes glared with the horrible vindictive look which I knew so well.

As I looked, the eyes saw the sinking sun, and the look of hate in them turned to triumph.

But on the instant, came the sweep and flash of Jonathan's great knife. I shrieked as I saw it shear through the throat; whilst at the same moment Mr. Morris's bowie knife plunged into the heart.

It was like a miracle, but before our very eyes, and almost in the drawing of a breath, the whole body crumbled into dust and passed from our sight.

Real Vampires

Despite his continuing popularity, Count Dracula is a fictitious character, and most people accept that human vampires do not exist. There is a vampire in the animal world, however, and it does subsist on blood. The vampire bat is a small bat, only 3 inches (8 centimeters) long, that lives in Central and South America. Because these bats have a very narrow esophagus, they can ingest only liquids. They use their razor-sharp, triangular front teeth to pierce the skin of sleeping cattle and other large mammals and drink their blood. Unlike Dracula, vampire bats do not suck blood but lap it up with their tongues in the same way that cats lap up milk.

Vampire bats do not normally attack humans but will do so if the opportunity presents itself. People in areas where there are vampire bats should keep their feet covered when sleeping. The bat will usually go for the exposed feet when coming across a sleeping person.

Humans bitten by a vampire bat don't have to worry about having all their blood drained by this tiny animal. Nor do they have to be concerned about turning into a vampire themselves. What is a concern is the diseases that the bat can spread to its victims, especially rabies.

STOKER'S MASTERPIECE

Dracula ranks as a classic of horror literature on several counts. First, Stoker made the rather audacious choice to set his tale of terror in the present. In contrast, most of the classic Gothic novels of the eighteenth and nineteenth centuries took place in the past, often set in crumbling

Even before Stoker's groundbreaking novel, vampires were gaining popularity among readers. This illustration accompanied a serial novel published in 1847.

medieval castles. While the novel begins in just such a gloomy castle in Transylvania, most of the action takes place in contemporary Whitby and London. Stoker had brought vampires into the real, everyday world that his readers inhabited, making the tale all the more chilling.

Second, Stoker took the daring step of keeping Count Dracula off-stage for most of the novel. After leaving his castle, he does not reappear, and then only briefly, until very near the end of the novel. His hold on Lucy, Mina, and the others is so powerful that his very absence makes him appear all the more omnipotent and mysterious. By the finale, he has become the very incarnation of evil.

Finally, Stoker's masterful intertwining of the vampire myth with sexual taboos has given Dracula's story overtones that resonate to this day. Dracula's attacks, sucking blood from the lily-white necks of Lucy and Mina, and the similar attempted assault on Harker by the three vampire women have heavy overtones of sexual seduction. These sexual tensions went completely unmentioned by the book's initial critics and readers.

THE CRITICS RESPOND

Completed by Stoker in 1896, *Dracula* was published the following May. The critical and public response to the novel was decidedly mixed. Some critics praised the book as a horror yarn but damned it as something less than a work of literature.

"*Dracula* is highly sensational," wrote a reviewer in *The Athenaeum,* "but it is wanting in the constructive art as well as in the higher literary sense. It reads at times like a mere series of grotesquely incredible events."

"This weird tale is about vampires, not a single, quiet creeping vampire, but a whole band of them . . . " wrote the *Punch* critic. "It is a pity that Mr. Bram Stoker was not content to employ such supernatural anti-vampire receipts [recipes] as his wildest imagination might have invented without venturing on a domain where angels fear to tread."

Stoker's fellow authors were generally less qualified in their praise. "I think it is the very best story of diablerie [devil's work] which I have read for many years," wrote his friend Arthur Conan Doyle. "It is really wonderful how with so much exciting intent over so long a book there is never an anticlimax."

A Mother's Opinion

Few initial readers of *Dracula* were as enthusiastic as was Charlotte Stoker, who became a social activist and spokesperson for the poor in middle age. Here is an excerpt from a letter she wrote to her son after she finished reading his most famous novel:

> My dear it is splendid, a thousand miles beyond anything you have written before, and I feel certain will place you very high in the writers of the day. . . . No book since Mrs. Shelley's "Frankenstein" or indeed any other at all has come near yours in originality, or terror—Poe is nowhere. I have read much but I have never met a book like it at all. In its terrible excitement it should make a widespread reputation and much money for you.

Charlotte's words were prophetic, but unfortunately *Dracula's* greatest success would not come in her or her son's lifetimes.

A MODEST SUCCESS

For all the interest it stirred up, *Dracula* was not the runaway best seller Stoker had hoped. The initial printing of three thousand copies did sell out, but the novel was only a modest success at first. In 1899, the publisher Doubleday & McClure came out with an American edition. By 1901, *Dracula* had been translated into French, German, and Icelandic, among other languages.

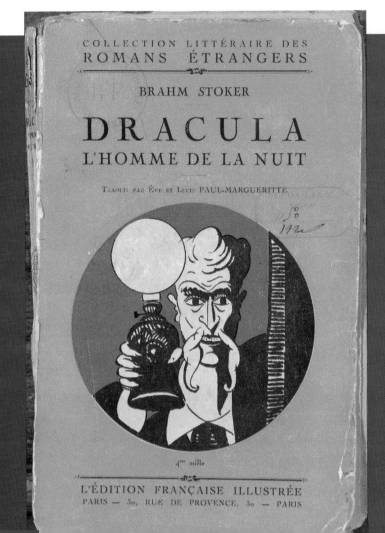

This French edition of *Dracula* was published in 1920. It was the second French edition published that year.

A STAGED READING

Being a man of the theater, Stoker had high hopes that Dracula would be a great success on the stage in play form. Immediately after its publication, he arranged for a reading at the Lyceum of a hasty adaptation he had written. He called his rather crude play version *Dracula: or The Un-Dead A Play in a Prologue and Five Acts.* The reading took place on a weekday morning and ran for four hours. The small audience consisted of actors, friends, and Stoker's cook. The role of Mina was played by Ellen Terry's daughter. It is possible that Stoker was anxious to get a play

Dracula did find success as a stage production, but not until after Stoker's death.

version mounted, regardless of its quality, simply to protect the copyright of a stage property.

The one person Stoker wanted to impress most with the reading was his boss, Henry Irving. He hoped the great actor would mount a production of the play at the Lyceum and star in it as Count Dracula. But when Stoker asked the actor what he thought when the reading ended, Irving is said to have bellowed, "Dreadful!"

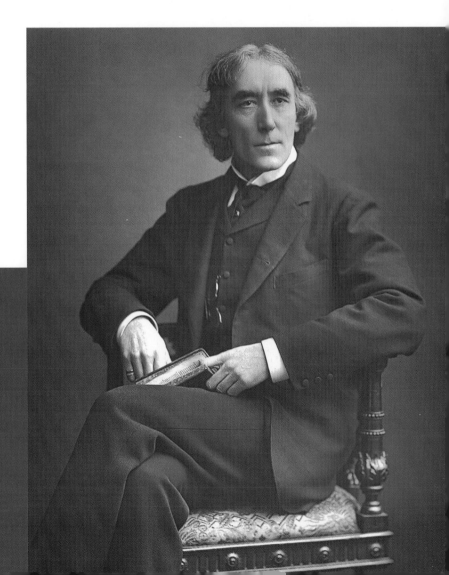

Henry Irving could be overbearing and cruel, even to his loyal friend.

Bela Lugosi found fame playing Count Dracula on Broadway.

Irving may have rejected Dracula for two reasons. He may have felt that Count Dracula got too little stage time and was too small a role for a star actor such as himself. It is also possible that the egotistical actor didn't want to admit to himself that Stoker, his theater manager, was a talented writer whose work was worthy of his theater company. Ironically, Irving passed on what could have been his greatest triumph. Today, Dracula is one of the most famous fictional characters in world literature, while Henry Irving is barely remembered outside his native England.

But the immediate consequences for Stoker were bitterly disappointing. The reading was the only stage production of his great work that he would see in his lifetime.

Dracula on the Stage

In 1924, Irish-born actor-manager Hamilton Deane, who had acted with Irving, was given permission by Florence Stoker to write and mount an adaptation of *Dracula*. Deane transformed Stoker's novel into an effective Victorian melodrama. What the story lost in subtlety it made up for in thrills. The play moved to London's West End in February 1927, where it was a huge hit with audiences, although the critics dismissed it. Deane, who played the role of Dr. Van Helsing, was an enthusiastic showman. According to the Stoker biographer Daniel Farson, he had a nurse stationed in the theater during performances in case anyone fainted from fright. At one performance twenty-nine people did.

A New York production was scheduled, but the producers had some qualms about Deane's script and brought in journalist John Balderston to beef it up for Broadway audiences. Again, the play was a smashing success, and the Deane-Balderston version has gone on to be a staple of repertory and summer stock companies on both sides of the Atlantic. Part of the success of the Broadway production was due to the unknown Hungarian actor who played the count. His name was Bela Lugosi.

In 1939, Deane played the role of Count Dracula in a Broadway production that fittingly was transferred to London's Lyceum. It was the next-to-last production in the theater that Bram Stoker once managed before it closed that same year. A Broadway revival of the play in 1977 starring Frank Langella as Count Dracula and featuring sets and costumes by illustrator and writer Edward Gorey was a huge hit. Stoker would have been very pleased by the stage success of his novel.

By the turn of the century, the Lyceum Theatre was struggling.

SEVEN

END OF
AN ERA

Despite his disappointment at Irving's refusal to consider Dracula for the Lyceum, Stoker continued to serve as the theater's general manager. He really had no choice. Florence's tastes were expensive, and Noel was enrolled in private school. There was no way Stoker could survive financially on his royalties as an author. Years of Irving's free spending on lavish productions had placed the theater in debt that grew steadily. Stoker did what he could to keep costs in line with the budget and hold the creditors at bay with polite letters, but the situation only grew worse with time.

TROUBLE AT THE LYCEUM

Several other unforeseen setbacks indicated that the Lyceum's—and Irving's—golden days were coming to an end. On February 18, 1898, a fire broke out in the theater's storage area that destroyed the scenery for forty-four productions. Soon after, while on tour in Scotland, Irving suffered a bout of pleurisy and pneumonia. He could not perform again for seven weeks.

But there was worse to come. While recovering from his illness, Irving felt weak and vulnerable. He agreed to sell the Lyceum to a syndicate, while he would continue to have artistic control as actor-manager. He had not bothered to consult either Stoker or his stage manager H. J. Loveday, before making the decision. Stoker was shocked when he heard the news of the impending sale, but nothing he or Loveday could say would change the actor's mind. He continued working for Irving but their relationship was never the same again.

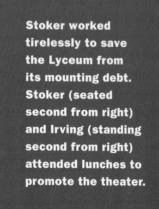

Stoker worked tirelessly to save the Lyceum from its mounting debt. Stoker (seated second from right) and Irving (standing second from right) attended lunches to promote the theater.

MORE NOVELS

When the company made its sixth U.S. tour in October 1899, Stoker was pleasantly surprised to see himself hailed by the American press not as the manager of Irving's theatrical company but as the author of *Dracula*. One enthusiastic journalist wrote, "[I]t is hard to imagine Bram Stoker a business manager, to say nothing of his possessing an imagination capable of projecting *Dracula* upon paper."

Stoker continued to write, setting the challenging goal of finishing a new novel every year. The results were often disappointing. *Miss Betty* (1898), which he dedicated to Florence, was a novel he had been working on when he started *Dracula*. A rare venture for the author into realistic domestic life, it was about a young woman who falls for a highwayman who only wants her money. It was quickly dismissed by critics as a weak effort, a judgment Stoker himself made years earlier when he put it aside. His next novel, *The Mystery of the*

Bram Stoker had a lot to be proud of, but also a lot to worry about, in the first years of the twentieth century.

Sea, published in 1902, was the prototype of the spy thriller and fared considerably better. That same year, the Lyceum, plagued by financial problems, closed, and Charlotte Stoker died at age eighty-three. Stoker continued to work as manager for Irving's productions elsewhere and on tour. In 1904, he published the novel *The Man,* another non-horror story about a woman searching for love with the right man. Stoker's empathy for the heroine, who defies convention, is impressive for a time period when women had few rights and were subjugated by men.

Stoker's Mummy Novel

Few admirers of *Dracula* are aware that its author also popularized the mummy genre in horror novels. *The Jewel of Seven Stars* (1903) is considered by many readers to be Stoker's best book after *Dracula.* One critic called it a "tale of mystery and imagination equal to anything that ever emerged from the fertile brain of Edgar Allan Poe."

It is about an archaeologist who, while exploring the tomb of an ancient Egyptian queen, finds a brilliant gem, the jewel of the title, on the mummy's hand. In the course of the novel, the long dead Queen Tara comes to possess the soul of the archaeologist's daughter. The original ending of the novel was shattering and tragic. A later edition, published after the author's death, has a happier ending. It is possible Stoker himself rewrote it at the request of his publisher. *The Jewel of Seven Stars* has been adapted to film twice as *Blood from the Mummy's Tomb* (1971) and *The Awakening* (1980), which starred Charlton Heston as the tormented archaeologist.

THE DEATH OF THE MASTER

Henry Irving continued to perform despite his declining health. On October 13, 1905, he was barely able to complete a performance of the play *Becket* at a London theater. Irving went from the theater to the Midland Hotel, where he collapsed in the lobby and died. Stoker arrived a few minutes later and closed the dead man's eyes. It was the last act he would perform for his employer. When the body was carried upstairs, Stoker went to work sending out countless telegrams to inform the press, family, and friends of the actor's death.

"It was all so desolate and lonely," he later wrote about Irving's death, "as so much of his life had been. So lonely that in the midst of my own sorrow I could not but rejoice at one thing: for him there was now Peace and Rest."

Irving's passing was seen as the end of an era in the English-speaking theater. All England mourned his death, and his ashes were buried in the Poets' Corner of Westminster Abbey. In his will Irving left nothing to Stoker, the man who had been his constant friend, faithful secretary, and loyal manager for twenty-seven years.

Henry Irving was buried in a corner of Westminster Abbey reserved for venerated writers and performing artists.

The death of Henry Irving (above) devastated Stoker, but he celebrated the life of his friend in a memoir published in 1906.

Final Years

Whatever mixed feelings Stoker had about the man he had devoted nearly thirty years of his life to, Irving's death was a devastating blow. Within a year Stoker suffered a stroke and was unconscious for a full day. The stroke left him unable to walk easily and seriously weakened his eyesight. He also suffered from Bright's disease, which affects the kidneys. At age fifty-seven, Bram Stoker's health was declining.

REMEMBERING IRVING

Still obsessed with the great actor who dominated his life, Stoker used what strength he had to write the memoir *Personal Reminiscences of Henry*

Irving, published in two volumes in 1906. The book was no frank review of his years with Irving but bordered on idolatry of the late actor. Stoker himself remained a minor character in the story, with some tantalizing glimpses of personal insight surfacing occasionally.

"Looking back I cannot honestly find any moment in my life when I failed him," he wrote, "or when I put myself forward in any way. In my own speaking to the dead man I can find an analogue in the words of heart-breaking sincerity:

> Stand up on the jasper sea
> And be witness I have given
> All the gifts required of me!"

The verse was taken from a poem by the English poet Elizabeth Barrett Browning. Stoker's Irving book sold well enough, but some critics complained about the lack of a more critical viewpoint. Like Count Dracula, Irving seemed to exert a power over his friend from beyond the

Elizabeth Barrett Browning and her husband, Robert Browning, were well-loved English poets in their time. They married when she was forty years old.

grave. Stoker, when his health permitted, traveled the country, lecturing about Irving and his legacy.

He worked only one more time in the theater. An American opera singer asked him to serve as business manager for his London production of a musical based on Oliver Goldsmith's novel *The Vicar of Wakefield*. The production was a disaster from the start. The adapter angered by cuts in his script, took his name off the program, and one of the leading players, the great Irish tenor John McCormack, left the show. It closed in two months.

LAST LITERARY EFFORTS

Stoker missed the companionship of his life in the theater and joined a writing society for the social contacts. In several articles, he wrote for *Nineteenth Century Magazine* in 1908, Stoker became a crusader for censorship in literature and denounced the sexual content of many contemporary novels.

"This article," he concluded in one piece, "is no mere protest against academic faults or breaches of good taste. It is a deliberate indictment of a class of literature so vile that it is actually corrupting the nation."

It seems very odd that the author of *Dracula*, a novel filled with not-so-hidden sexual content, should end his career as a puritanical prude. A moral man in every way, Stoker may not have been fully conscious of the sexual undertones of *Dracula* and other of his horror novels. It is also possible that his criticism of popular novelists was fueled in part by envy. After all, they had become rich from their writing, and he hadn't.

Sir Arthur Conan Doyle is famous for creating Sherlock Holmes. Like Stoker, he was interested in the occult and even participated in séances.

Desperate for cash, Stoker continued to write at every opportunity. He produced a series of profiles for the newspaper the *New York World.* Among his subjects were his good friends Sir Arthur Conan Doyle and W. S. Gilbert, as well as the young British politician Winston Churchill, who would go on to become prime minister. Among the last books he published were a nonfiction work, *Famous Imposters,* and a collection of stories titled *Snowbound: The Record of a Theatrical Touring Party.* This interesting work was based on stories and anecdotes told by members of the Lyceum company while on tour. The framework of the collection was that the stories were all told while the company was snowbound in a train.

Stoker's last two novels were in the horror genre, both featuring women villains. *The Lady of the Shroud* was an unconvincing tale about a woman pretending to be a vampire. Of far greater interest is *The Lair of the White Worm,* his last novel, published in 1911, which he wrote in three months.

THE LAIR OF THE WHITE WORM

Of Stoker's eighteen published books, none is as bizarre as his last, *The Lair of the White Worm.* Young Adam Salton, the novel's protagonist, returns to his family estate in rural England. Among his neighbors is the mysterious widow Lady Arabella March, who dresses in white and whose approach frightens away snakes. Salton eventually comes to the astonishing conclusion that Lady Arabella is no lady at all, but a legendary local monster in disguise, a huge white worm that has lurked underground for two thousand years.

The book's plot and dialogue are at times laughable but entertaining. At one point Salton confides in a friend, "I never thought this fighting of an antediluvian monster would be such a complicated job." In the climax, Lady Arabella and her home are blown to smithereens by dynamite and sink into a hole in the earth. "[T]he seething contents of the hole rose, after the manner of a bubbling spring," wrote Stoker, "and Adam saw part of the thin form of Lady Arabella forced to the top amid a mass of slime, and what looked as if it had been a monster torn into shreds."

This outlandish tale has become Stoker's most popular book after *Dracula.* The English filmmaker Ken Russell made a film adaptation based very loosely on the novel in 1989 that is even more bizarre than the book.

THE END

Stoker suffered a second stroke in 1910. That same year Noel, his only child, became a chartered accountant and married. Unable to work, Stoker relied on the generosity of friends for money, such as novelist Hall Caine, to whom he had dedicated *Dracula*. Caine, unlike Stoker, was a phenomenally successful writer.

Although Hall Caine was a popular novelist in his lifetime, he rarely is read today.

HALL CAINE

"To My Dear Friend Hommy-Beg," reads the dedication Stoker wrote for *Dracula*. Few readers knew at the time that "Hommy-Beg" means "Little Tommy" in Manx, a Celtic language spoken on the Isle of Man in the Irish Sea. It was the nickname of Stoker's friend Hall Caine.

Thomas Henry Hall Caine was more than a good friend to Stoker. He was his literary mentor and adviser. Although six years younger than Stoker, Caine was a far more successful novelist.

Hall was raised in the city of Liverpool but spent part of his youth on the Isle of Man, where his uncle and aunt were farmers. The rustic, simple life on the island appealed to Caine, and he set some of his best-known novels there. *The Manxman* (1894), his first big seller, sold nearly 400,000 copies. *The Eternal City* (1901), set in Rome, sold more than one million copies worldwide. Caine was also a successful playwright who wrote an adaptation of "The Flying Dutchman" legend for Irving and his Lyceum Theatre. Irving played a ship's captain who defies God and is condemned to sail the seas in a phantom ship for eternity.

A devoutly religious person, Caine's novel *The Christian* (1897) is based on the parable of the Prodigal Son. His last work, published seven years after his death, was *Life of Christ* (1938).

In his prime, Caine was one of the most popular writers in the English language and a celebrity who was often seen in the company of kings and presidents. Today, he and his books are all but forgotten, while Bram Stoker, his less successful friend, is still read and is far more famous.

In February 1911, Stoker received a grant of one hundred pounds from the Royal Literary Fund. Unable to afford to live in their apartment in fashionable Chelsea, the Stokers moved to a small apartment in a less expensive part of London.

Just as Henry Irving overshadowed Stoker in life, so a tragedy of immense proportions overshadowed him in death. On April 15, 1912, the British luxury liner *Titanic* sank in the North Atlantic on its maiden voyage after striking an iceberg. The disaster and the subsequent investigation were still making headlines five days later when Bram Stoker, sick and exhausted at age sixty-four, died at home, his wife and son by his side. He was cremated, and his ashes buried at Golders Green Crematorium in London.

The *London Times'* obituary admitted that Stoker was "the master of a particularly lurid and creepy kind of fiction," but mentioned *Dracula* only briefly. It predicted that "his chief literary memorial will be his Reminiscences of Irving [which] . . . cannot but remain a valuable record of the workings of genius as they appeared to his devoted associate and admirer."

The *Pittsburgh Gazette* may have come to a better appreciation of Stoker's character, if not his achievement: "He was the finest and most tactful man that ever kept watch and ward at the gateway to stage greatness and reserve."

Of the eighteen books Stoker wrote in his lifetime, only one would survive him and take on a diabolical life of its own. Bram Stoker was dead, but Count Dracula, king of the undead, was just beginning his long and notorious career.

THE TITANIC DISASTER

The real-life horror of the sinking of the *Titanic* made the fictional horrors of *Dracula* pale by comparison. The largest ship in the world at 882.5 feet (269 meters) and described in one report as "practically unsinkable," *Titanic* sailed on its maiden voyage from England in early April 1912. It struck an iceberg about 1,600 miles (2,575 km) northeast of New York City, its final destination. The "unsinkable" *Titanic* sank in just two and half hours. Of about 2,200 passengers, only 705 survived. Among those who died were captains of industry and prominent social figures, as well as many of the poorest passengers, riding in steerage. Many more would have survived if the ship had an adequate number of lifeboats or if a vessel only 10 miles (16 km) away had responded to telegraph signals calling for help.

The *Titanic* tragedy resulted in better safety at sea. Strict rules were passed for the number of lifeboats that had to be present on vessels, and constant patrols were sent out to spot icebergs in well-traveled waters. The *Titanic* lives on in the public's imagination through a continuing stream of books, magazine articles, and movies. The exploration of the ship itself, which is slowly disintegrating on the ocean floor, continues.

1897 *Dracula*, the novel, is published.

1922 *Nosferatu*, a German film adaptation, is released.

1927 The play *Dracula* by Hamilton Deane and John Balderston opens on Broadway.

1931 The Hollywood film *Dracula*, starring Bela Lugosi, is released.

1936 Gloria Holden plays a descendant of the count in *Dracula's Daughter*.

1943 Lon Chaney Jr., stars as the count in *Son of Dracula*.

1944 John Carradine plays Dracula in *House of Frankenstein*.

1945 John Carradine plays Dracula in *House of Dracula*.

1958 *Horror of Dracula*, the first Dracula film in color, is released in England starring Christopher Lee.

1977 *Dracula* is revived on Broadway starring Frank Langella.

1992 *Bram Stoker's Dracula*, directed by Francis Ford Coppola, is released with Gary Oldman as Dracula.

2004 *Van Helsing* pits a youthful vampire hunter against the count.

Gary Oldman (bottom right) in *Bram Stoker's Dracula* has quite a different look from Frank Langella's handsome count (top left)!

NINE

Dracula Lives!

Florence Stoker proved a tireless promoter and protector of her husband's literary estate. In 1914, *Dracula's Guest and Other Weird Stories,* a collection of stories Stoker had been putting together when he died, was published. The title story had been the original first chapter of Dracula and described Jonathan Harker's strange coach journey to Transylvania on Walpurgis Night, the Witches' Sabbath. Stoker's publishers cut it from the novel because they felt the book was too long.

A CONTROVERSIAL ADAPTATION

Movies were still in their infancy when *Dracula* was published in 1897. By the time of Stoker's death, however, the silent film was well established as a form of entertainment and was on its way to becoming an art form. Early filmmakers often turned to literary works for their inspiration, and *Dracula,* with its sensational horrors, was a natural candidate for the screen.

The first film adaptation of *Dracula* was a Hungarian production that has unfortunately been lost. No prints of it have survived. In 1922, a German studio, Prana, mounted a production under the direction of the gifted director F. W. (Friedrich Wilhelm) Murnau. The film was called *Nosferatu: A Symphony of Horror.* The word "nosferatu" means "undead" in German.

There was a very good reason why Murnau did not call his film *Dracula.* The studio did not have the funds to pay for the rights to Stoker's novel but decided to go ahead and make its film anyway. Although the movie is obviously based on the novel, Murnau was careful to alter the plot, setting, and the characters' names. Count Dracula, for example, is called Count Orlok. The character of the madman Renfield has become the real estate agent Knock, who sends Hutter (Harker) to Dracula's castle.

When word of the film reached England, Florence Stoker sued the studio for adapting her husband's novel without permission. She eventu-

Max Schreck played Count Orlok, clearly based on Count Dracula, in the 1922 film *Nosferatu.*

ally won, and the suit bankrupted Prana Studio. As part of the settlement, Prana was ordered to destroy all prints of *Nosferatu*. Fortunately, some prints survived. *Nosferatu* is a cinema classic, arguably the greatest film adaptation of *Dracula* ever made.

Nosferatu—The German Dracula

F.W. Murnau was already a leading German film director when he made *Nosferatu*. Murnau's expressive use of shadows, natural locations, and a mobile camera heightened the mystery and terror of Stoker's story. Perhaps the most incredible feature of the film is its star, character actor Max Schreck, who played the vampire, Count Orlok. His surname in German, means "fright." Schreck's skeletal frame; his long, spidery fingers; and elongated head were truly frightening. Physically, he surpassed Stoker's own description of Dracula in horror. Several scenes from the film are unforgettably eerie, such as when Orlok literally pops up out of his coffin in the hold of the ship bound for his new home.

Murnau went on to make a fascinating film version of *Faust* (1926), based on the legend of a man who sells his soul to the devil. He moved to Hollywood in 1927, where he made several classic silent films. *Sunrise: A Song of Two Humans* (1927), the story of a husband and wife who rediscover their love after he has a brief affair, has been praised as one of the finest silent films ever made. *Tabu* (1931), his second sound film, was an intriguing blend of documentary and fictional filmmaking set in the South Seas. One week after its premier, Murnau died tragically at age forty-two in an automobile accident.

Above is the movie poster for the 1931 classic film *Dracula* with Bela Lugosi in the title role and Helen Chandler starring as Mina.

LUGOSI AND COMPANY

When Hollywood's Universal Studios decided to film *Dracula* in 1931, it went through the proper legal channels. The studio paid $40,000—a fortune at the time—to Stoker's estate for the rights to the novel, although its film was based on the Deane-Balderston play adaptation. The Hungarian actor Bela Lugosi and Edward van Sloan, who played Van Helsing on Broadway, both reprised their stage roles in the film. Unlike *Nosferatu,* Universal's *Dracula* was slow, stage-bound, and lacking in visual excitement. Only Lugosi's legendary performance as Dracula makes it a classic. His stiff aristocratic bearing, hypnotic stare, and thick Hungarian accent remain the definitive trademarks of the Transylvanian vampire.

Despite its failings, the film *Dracula* created a sensation on its first release and began the cycle of classic horror films for which Universal Studios is still known today. Dracula would quickly be followed by such screen monsters as Frankenstein, the Mummy, and the Wolf

The success of Universal's *Dracula* is mostly because of the hypnotic appeal of its star, Bela Lugosi.

Man. Interestingly, Lugosi only played Dracula once more on film, seventeen years later in *Abbott and Costello Meet Frankenstein* (1948), an entertaining mixture of comedy and horror.

BELA LUGOSI

The son of a banker, Bela Lugosi studied acting at the Budapest Academy of Theatrical Arts in his native Hungary. He had a successful career on stage and was starting to make films when a communist takeover caused him to flee his homeland in 1919. Lugosi emigrated to the United States two years later. After his great success on stage and screen as Count Dracula, Lugosi turned down the role of Frankenstein's monster in *Frankenstein* because he would be unrecognizable under all the heavy makeup and would have no lines to speak. The part went to Boris Karloff, who became Lugosi's rival for the title of Hollywood's king of horror. The two actors were paired in a series of horror movies at Universal, including *The Black Cat* (1934), *The Raven* (1935), and *The Invisible Ray* (1936).

Unlike Karloff, however, Lugosi quickly lost his star status because of his poor judgment in choosing roles and a difficult temperament. One of his last good roles was Ygor, the vengeful hunchback who befriends Karloff's Frankenstein monster in the classic *Son of Frankenstein* (1939). He reprised the role in *The Ghost of Frankenstein* (1942). After that Lugosi was largely stuck in grade-B horror movies playing mad scientists and second-rate vampires. His later years were plagued by financial problems and drug addiction. In 1955 he committed himself to the California State Hospital for his addiction. When he died in August 1956, his family had him buried in his Dracula cape.

Through the 1930s and 1940s, Dracula and his offspring would appear in such Universal films as *Dracula's Daughter* (1936), supposedly based on "Dracula's Guest"; *Son of Dracula* (1943), in which Lon Chaney Jr. donned the cape; and the multimonster fests *House of Frankenstein* (1944) and *House of Dracula* (1945). John Carradine, who played the count in these last two films, was a cadaverous and dapper Count Dracula, dressed in top hat and tails. This image was considerably closer to Stoker's conception of the character than Lugosi had been. By the mid-1940s, horror films went into decline, and Dracula and the other classic monsters went into semiretirement. But you can't keep a good vampire in his coffin forever.

In *House of Dracula,* John Carradine played the stylish count opposite Martha O'Driscoll.

A NEW AND BLOODIER COUNT

It was Bela Lugosi's dream to star in a color remake of *Dracula*. Two years after his death, England's Hammer Studios released *Horror of Dracula* (1958) in color, and a new star of horror films was born. Christopher Lee was a young, tall, strikingly handsome Count Dracula. The film was noted for its impressive period sets and graphic violence. While even a drop of blood was scarcely seen in the old Universal Dracula films, *Horror of Dracula* showed plenty of bright red blood. Dr. Van Helsing in the British film was played by the British actor Peter Cushing who would become as big a star in horror movies as Lee. They would often co-star in the same horror movie, much as Karloff and Lugosi had two decades before. Over the next sixteen years Lee played Dracula in a string of Hammer sequels, each more gory than the last.

"It [Count Dracula] is one of the greatest parts ever created, one of the most famous and fantastic . . ." Lee has said. "No actor can ask more."

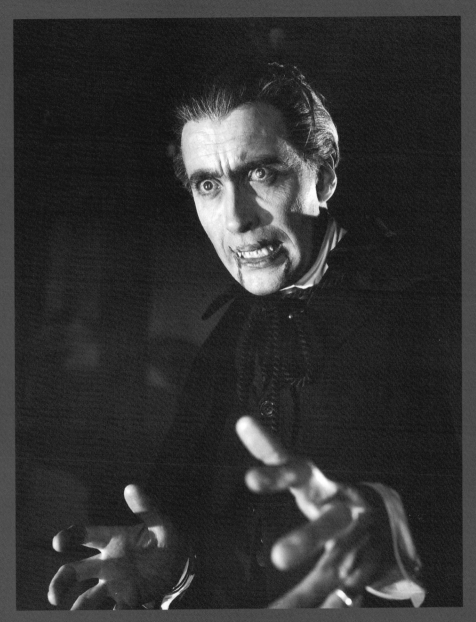

In 1977, Christopher Lee published his autobiography, entitled *Tall, Dark, and Gruesome.*

Christopher Lee

No actor has played Dracula more times on film than Christopher Lee. He was born in London in 1922 and worked as an office clerk in a shipping company before serving as a pilot in the Royal Air Force (RAF) during World War II. Returning to civilian life, Lee became an actor, playing many small roles in British films. Stardom finally came when he began working for Hammer Films. Lee convincingly portrayed Frankenstein's monster, the mummy, and later the evil Dr. Fu Manchu. Since then he had played both good and villainous roles in scores of films, including the assassin Scaramanga in the James Bond film *The Man with the Golden Gun* (1974). A new generation of filmgoers has enjoyed his performances as the evil Saruman the White in *The Lord of the Rings* trilogy and as *Count Dooku* in the most recent Star Wars films.

    Lee has had this to say about Count Dracula's continuing popularity with readers and moviegoers: "He offers the illusion of immortality, the subconscious wish we all have for limitless power . . . a man of tremendous brain and physical strength . . . he is either a reincarnation or he has never died. He is a superman image, with erotic appeal for women who find him totally alluring. In many ways, he is everything people would like to be—the anti-hero, the heroic villain. . . . He is part saint, part sinner."

Christopher Lee has played Dracula in ten different movies!

A DRACULA FOR EVERY OCCASION

By the 1970s, Dracula had become a familiar friend to moviegoers and an icon of popular culture. Variations on Stoker's classic count abounded. There was a black Dracula (*Blacula*), a senior-citizen Dracula (*Old Dracula*), a western Dracula (*Billy the Kid vs. Dracula*), a corporate executive Dracula (*The Satanic Rites of Dracula*), a romantic Dracula (*Dracula* starring Frank Langella), and comic Draculas (*Love at First Bite* and *Dracula—Dead and Loving It,* directed by Mel Brooks).

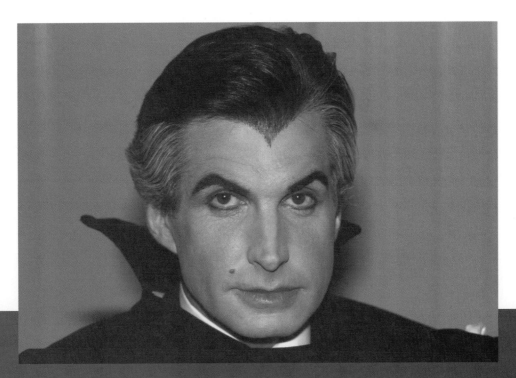

In *Love at First Bite*, George Hamilton plays Count Dracula searching for love—and blood—in New York City.

In 1992, the celebrated filmmaker Francis Ford Coppola made *Bram Stoker's Dracula*. The stellar cast included Gary Oldman as the count, Anthony Hopkins as Van Helsing, Winona Ryder as Mina, and Keanu Reeves as Jonathan Harker. Coppola's film was visually bold and exciting but was not as faithful to the novel as the title suggests.

More recently, filmmakers have taken even greater liberties with Stoker's novel. In the lavish *Van Helsing* (2004), the middle-aged vampire hunter has been transformed into a dashing young adventurer played by Hugh Jackman. Van Helsing's bloody struggle with Count Dracula also brought back to active duty the Wolf Man and Frankenstein's monster.

As a salute to Stoker, Coppola included an advertisement for the Lyceum Theatre in his 1992 movie. Here, Gary Oldman, as Dracula, confronts Keanu Reeves.

The Transylvanian blood-sucker has become one of the most-filmed fictitious characters in history, second only to detective Sherlock Holmes. But film is not the only entertainment media to embrace the count.

DRACULA FOREVER

Everywhere you look in popular culture, you will find Stoker's indestructible count lurking in the shadows. He has been celebrated in television series, comic books, cartoon gags, commercials, and dolls and models. There is even a Dracula cereal called *Count Chocula* and a frozen ice pop that advertised itself with the words "Count Dracula's Deadly Secret—Eat One Before Sunset!"

There are several international societies devoted to Dracula, vampires, and Gothic literature and movies. They are the Transylvanian Society of Dracula, the Count

Bram Stoker's most famous creation lives on in the popular imagination, especially on Halloween. Even a vampire can have a sweet tooth!

Sighisoara, the birthplace of Vlad Tepes, has become a tourist attraction for those fascinated by the fictional Dracula.

Dracula Society, the Vampire Empire, the Vampire Information Exchange, and Vampire Studies. The London chapter of the Count Dracula Society placed a plaque on the London residence of Bram Stoker to commemorate the writer.

There are also several organizations dedicated to Bram Stoker and his work. They included the Bram Stoker Memorial Association, the Bram Stoker Society, and Stoker's Dracula Organisation, which operates an annual summer school in Clontarf, Ireland, Stoker's birthplace. *Dracula's* author has also been honored by the Horror Writers Association, which has since 1987 presented the annual Bram Stoker Awards for Superior Achievement in all genres of horror. Among the celebrities who have received the Life Achievement Stoker Award are fantasy and horror writers Ray Bradbury, Stephen King, and Anne Rice, and actor Christopher Lee.

Romania, home to Transylvania and Vlad Dracul, has cashed in on the Dracula craze by offering packaged tours of Dracula country. The Transylvanian Society boasts of its "definitive Dracula tour." Thrill-seeking tourists follow in the footsteps of Jonathan Harker and even spend a night at the Count Dracula Hotel, where they can attend a masked ball and buy some of "Count Dracula's treasures." More authentic Dracula tours take tourists to the ruins of Vlad Tepes's actual castle. There they can walk up about 1,500 steps to see the castle's dusty remains.

In 2004, construction began in Snagov, Romania, on the ultimate Dracula attraction, Dracula Land, a Dracula theme park. Snagov is thought to be the burial place of Vlad Dracul. The park, co-sponsored by the Romanian government, has been highly criticized by preservationists and environmentalists who feel a theme park will harm the historical and natural beauty of the region and cheapen the memory of Vlad, a national hero in Romania for defending his land from the Turks. Meanwhile, another Romanian town, Brasnov, has unveiled plans for its own competing theme park—Empire Dracula.

More than a century after he first appeared in print, Count Dracula continues to haunt our dreams and imagination. The writer Leonard Wolf calls him "something of a cultural hero whom our first duty it is to hate even while we have for him a certain weird admiration. . . . How strong, how graceful, how lonely, how wise. And above all—and here is the central mystery—how deadly . . . and erotic."

Bram Stoker drew on many facets of his life to create his masterpiece, which has not been out of print since its first publication. These influences included his lonely and bedridden childhood, the bloody and supernatural stories his mother told him, the lore of the vampire, and his relationship with the overbearing Henry Irving. In *Dracula,* all these influences come together to create a novel of great terror and beauty that plumbs the mysteries of life, love, and death.

Count Dracula is as attractive as he is repulsive—a villain we love to hate. Bram Stoker's undead legacy is sure to live on.

TIMELINE

BRAM STOKER'S LIFE   **WORLD EVENTS**

1847 Abraham (Bram) Stoker is born in Clontarf, Ireland, on November 8.

The Irish Potato Famine reaches its climax, killing about 750,000 people.

1863 Stoker enters Trinity College, Dublin.

1871 Stoker graduates from Trinity College and enters the civil service in Dublin as a clerk. Stoker begins to review plays for *The Dublin Evening Mail.*

1872 Stoker's first short story, "The Crystal Cup," is published in *London Society* magazine.

1876 Stoker's father, Abraham, dies in Italy on October 12. Stoker changes his first name to Bram. He reviews Henry Irving's portrayal of Hamlet in a Dublin production, and the two become friends.

1878 Stoker marries Florence Balcombe on December 4.

1879 Stoker becomes general manager of the Lyceum Theatre under Irving. His only child, Noel, is born on December 31.

1881 Stoker publishes his first full-length work of fiction, *Under the Sunset,* a collection of children's stories.

1883 Stoker makes his first visit to the United States with Irving's touring company.

1890 Stoker's first novel, *The Snake's Pass,* is published. He begins work on *Dracula.*

1897 *Dracula* is published in May.

1898 The Spanish-American War breaks out.

1903 Stoker publishes *The Jewel of Seven Stars,* his mummy novel.

1905 Henry Irving dies on October 13.

1906 Stoker suffers a stroke.

1911 Stoker publishes his last novel, *The Lair of the White Worm.*

1912 The ocean liner *Titanic* sinks on April 15.

Bram Stoker dies on April 20 at age sixty four.

1914 *Dracula's Guest and Other Weird Stories* is published posthumously.

To Find Out More

BOOKS

Pipe, Jim. *In the Footsteps of Dracula*. Brookfield, CT: Copper Beech Books, 1995.

Skal, David J. *Hollywood Gothic: The Tangled Web of Dracula from Novel to Stage to Screen*. New York: Faber and Faber, 2004.

Stoker, Bram. *Dracula.* New York: Signet Books, 1997.

Whitelaw, Nancy. *Bram Stoker: Author of Dracula*. Greensboro, NC: Morgan Reynolds, Inc., 2004.

VIDEOS AND DVDS

The Awakening (1980). Warner Home Video, VHS, 2001.

Dracula—The Legacy Collection. Universal Video, DVD, 2004. (Boxed set includes *Dracula,* the Spanish version of *Dracula, Dracula's Daughter, Son of Dracula,* and *House of Dracula.*)

Horror of Dracula (1958). Warner Home Video, DVD, 2004.

Nosferatu (1922). Image Entertainment, DVD, 2002.

ORGANIZATIONS AND ONLINE SITES

The Bram Stoker Memorial Association
Penthouse North, Suite 145
29 Washington Square West
New York, NY 10011-9180
http://www.benecke.com/stoker.html

This is the world's largest, most active Stoker society. The association is based in New York City's historic Greenwich Village.

The Bram Stoker Society
c/o David Lass
Regent House, Trinity College
Dublin 2, Ireland

This is the oldest Stoker society, founded in 1980.

Stoker's Dracula Organisation
http://www.bramstokercentre.org

The goal of this society is to gain greater recognition for Bram Stoker by way of the Stoker Memorial/Resource/Cultural Heritage Centre in Clontarf. The site has biographical information on Stoker and Count Dracula and sponsors an annual summer school.

A Note on Sources

While literally hundreds of books have been written about Count Dracula—the novel, the fictional character, and the historical figure—until quite recently little attention has been given to the book's author, Bram Stoker. Stoker's own reticence about his life in his own writings has made the biographer's task all the more difficult. The only biography of the author for children currently in print is Nancy Whitelaw's *Bram Stoker: Author of Dracula*. While she is quite good about discussing Stoker's early life and his experiences in the theater, Whitelaw gives little insight into Stoker the writer and the significance of *Dracula* as a horror novel.

Among adult biographies, Daniel Farson's *The Man Who Wrote Dracula: A Biography of Bram Stoker* is lively and entertaining. Farson was Stoker's great-nephew and was himself a colorful character. The reminiscences gleaned from relatives and friends are insightful and fascinating. A more definitive, scholarly biography is Barbara Belford's *Bram Stoker: A Biography of the Author of Dracula*. It goes into great depth about Stoker's career at the Lyceum and his relationship with Henry Irving. At times Stoker's story gets lost in Irving's, although Belford is extremely good at drawing perceptive parallels between Stoker's life and experiences and *Dracula*.

An excellent introduction to the "real" Dracula, Vlad Tepes, and his connection to Bram Stoker's fictional character is *In Search of Dracula: The History of Dracula and Vampires* by Raymond T. McNally and Radu Florescu. Originally published in the early 1970s, it was updated in 1994 by the authors. *Dracula Scrapbook,* edited by Peter Haining, is a lively and entertaining cornucopia of facts and folklore about Dracula, Stoker, and vampires in film and literature.

Among all the many editions of Dracula, the best is *The Essential Dracula,* edited and exhaustively annotated by Leonard Wolf. The finest of Stoker's short horror stories have been collected in *Best Ghost and Horror Stories.* It includes such chillers as "The Squaw," "The Dualitists," "Burial of the Rats," "The Judge's House," and "Dracula's Guest."

—*Steven Otfinoski*

INDEX

About the Author

Steven Otfinoski has written more than one hundred books for young adults and children. He has written numerous biographies about presidents, explorers, writers, and scientists. He has also written books about countries, states, history, creative writing, and public speaking. For adults he has published two books on rock music.

Otfinoski lives in Connecticut with his wife, Beverly, a teacher and editor, and their two children, Daniel and Martha. When he's not writing, he enjoys playing tennis, watching movies, listening to and collecting all kinds of music, and reading nonfiction.